For Jerry

Thank you
Friendship
& Support

Poems
from an Unending
Pandemic

Phillip

9/14/2022

Word on the Street

Phillip Giambri's collection *Poems from an Unending Pandemic* captures, with brutal emotional honesty and unexpected biting humor, the searing heartbreak and infuriating injustice of 2020. He takes us through those early days of abrupt lockdown (and the ensuing body count) to the outrageous injustice of George Floyd's murder and the BLM protests that followed. His service as a submariner never stops him from calling out America on its bullshit and selfishness. And he never turns his back on his country, his passion for expression, his loyalty to his hometown, and his fierce love for his friends and lovers. – C. O. Moed, Writer, Poet

Philip Giambri's book of poems is a wake-up call. He addresses the problems in America with language that is blunt in a message that is sharply on point. His poetry speaks to the heart and mind and I highly recommend his book. -Evelyn Kandel, Nassau County Poet Laureate. 2019-2022

Poems
from an Unending
Pandemic

by
Phillip Giambri

Published in the United States 2020
by
Pink Trees Press
New York

Dedicated
to the Lady whose love
brought light
to the terrible darkness
of this pandemic
and
to my East Village neighbors
at our food pantries
whose generosity
and open hearts
helped us all survive.

Introduction

After months of lockdown in a pandemic malaise, I awoke one morning and began writing poems that I dated and posted on Facebook. I had no idea at the time how many poems would emerge or why they happened. It seemed to be my way of dealing with the isolation, loneliness, and depression of the high daily death count in New York City. These poems were my relief valve and I hope that the feelings and emotions expressed are part of a national shared experience and that they may touch others.

Table of Contents

BLM

(06/02/2020)

I am this time.
This time is mine.
You were not my voice.
I am my voice now
I will be heard
and this time
you will listen.

Dreamers

(06/06/2020)

How did we get to this place?

We were a nation of dreamers
a nation of idealists
a nation of accomplishment
a nation that valued rule of law.

But we are also a nation
that dreams only white dreams.
a nation based on consumerism not need
a nation based on capitalism not charity
a nation that values the rule of law
but not for all.

We are not the United States
imagined by our founders
but we can be
if we start again
and dream a different dream
a dream more fair.

These Times

(06/14/2020)

Dreadin' these times
yet wedded to these times.
We shook the bottle 'til it blew up
and we still ain't grew up.

Now we screamin' at the system
that we allowed to become us
'til it's eaten the core of us
yet we all still suckin' on its tit.

We are not the victims,
we are the cause.
We've been bought, sold,
and delivered
to the highest bidder
while Mitch the Bitch
spins the wheel
and everybody loses.

Identity Theft

(06/25/2020)

Months of isolation, distancing,
lack of interaction with others,
watching daily death tolls
mount into absurdity
and catastrophic national
political failures
eventually caused me
to emotionally disconnect;
for self-preservation, I guess.

No new life experiences
other than loneliness and despair
have slowly eaten into my identity
and the perception of who I am.

Music and photos
were always a means of
connecting to memories
and emotions
but they now seem detached
as though they were someone else's

or that I read about
or saw in a movie or play.
I still see them in my mind
or in pictures
but they no longer belong to me
or connect emotionally.

When this pandemic ends
and life enters a new "normal"
will I emerge with a new identity,
bereft of past life experiences
beginning life anew
at 79 years old?

I hope that as I emerge from isolation
and engage with others
in the new reality
that I will be able to reconnect
to the me that was
and enjoy the memories of past life
experiences, emotions, and loves
once again.

TIME TO SCREAM!

(06/28/2020)

I'm mean, REALLY?
Masks are a political choice?
You're in the Red Zone
of ideological ignorance.
Real people are dying
and you choose no mask?

REALLY?
ARE YOU THAT UNCARING?

The First Amendment
to the Constitution
never anticipated that assholes
would choose going for haircuts
over saving the lives
 of older neighbors.

Don't ever dare to talk again
about "right to Life"
when you're okay

with killing me
Mother Fucker!

Grimm's Fairytale 2020

(06/30/2020)

Four months into it
sittin' on the couch
in your underwear and bathrobe
unwashed for five days now
watching the world fall apart on TV
belchin', fartin', and pickin'
at that new pimple on your cheek
wonderin' what the fuck happened
to romance,
dancin' close to soft music,
makin' out in a dark doorway,
feeling like your heart
was gonna' burst with joy,
smokin' a doobie,
watchin' a blazin' sunset on the pier.

life was full of possibilities,
we were all gonna be one,
we were gonna save the world.

Yeah, you remember that,

but that was another life
or maybe it never was.

Tinder 2020

(07/01/2020)

Hi, I'm Robin
I'm 27 years old
I'm 5' 7"
I used to be a blonde
I used to be a size 4
I used to be a Travel Agent
I used to go to night school
I used to love going to Yankee games
I used to hang in bars
I on Amsterdam Avenue
I used to jog in Central Park
I used to go to concerts
I used to love dining out
I used to love sex with the right guy
I used to pleasure myself
'til my vibrator broke
I used............ HE SWIPES LEFT

Hi, I'm Lloyd
I'm 30 years old
I'm 6' 2"

I used to work for City Tours
I used to work out four days a week
I used to have washboard abs
I used to love going to Mets games
I used to love rock concerts
I used to love hangin' with my buds
I used to love one-night stands
I used to love giving a woman
a screaming orgasm
I used to feel like a sex machine
I used to enjoy solo sex too
but porn got boring
I used to . . . . . SHE SWIPES LEFT

Pandemic Poem

(07/02/2020)

I was a story
now I'm a poem.
Life is too short
for flowery adjectives and adverbs
just stickin' to nouns and verbs.
Keepin' it real.

Blind Faith

(07/03/2020)

We thought we were all starring
in *Groundhog Day 2020*
and it was supposed to be a comedy
with a moral message.
We were wrong.

We're locked in reruns
of *Friday the 13th*
Trump is Jason
and lots of people are dying
'cause just like all horror movies,
the victims never pay attention
to the obvious script clues.
It's not funny, kids.
Blind faith kills.

Hope
On the Suicide of a Friend's Son
(07/21/2020)

Hope seems all that remains
in this dystopian night.
Peace and love are vanished, gone,
each of us now somehow broken
emotionally, physically, mentally,
no longer with means
to heal ourselves
from an unending panic
of aloneness.

We struggle,
gathering broken pieces
of the we that was us
but pieces seem missing or
no longer fit
the us that was we.

Only hope offers solace
or possibility
of redemption.

Reach for my hand.
I will be there for you
when you call out
alone in the night.

Love is gone,
only hope remains.

Let us hope together
that we can make the pieces fit
as one again
and may God once again
bless the America that was.

Unbroken

(07/26/2020)

I stand naked in the night
unbroken by the wind.
I am the windmill
I am Don Quixote!

Defiant Protest

(07/27/2020)

John: "Hey Mariner,
you need to write a pandemic poem
about lockdown masturbation.
Everybody can relate to that."

Me: Sequestered acts
of solo masturbation
are an anarchist's defiant protest
against a government
jerking us off
with COVID19 briefings.

John: WTF?

Artist Under Siege

(07/29/2020)

I am no longer.
I am disappeared;
somehow vanished
in a pandemic wilderness
of chaos and opposition.

I am no longer a poet.
Words have failed me.
Truth no longer exists.

I am no longer an artist.
Vision obscured
by bodies in freezer trucks.

I am no longer a dancer.
Movement obstructed
by Brown Shirt troops
and marching moms.

I am no longer an actor.
My stage now an ER
littered with unnamed
broken and dying.

I am no longer a musician.
My soft mellow notes
replaced by the screech
of sirens in the night.

I am no longer a singer.
My voice overtaken
by the wail of families
for the lost and gone.

All that remains of me
is one sound;
a single note:
an Aum of peace,
lost in the chaos
of dying dreams
and opposition anger.

We are Myth

(07/31/2020)

Could it be
that we are in actuality
ancient myths
of our native people
projected forward
as a cautionary tale
to their youth
on the consequences
of worshipping
an orange idol
and the resulting bat's plague?

Did we not see the return
of the white buffalo?
She was to be our guide.

Walking Dead

(08/22/2020)

Song lyrics of the 60s and 70s
led us to a new reality.
We were changing the world.
We failed.

Was it Disco that killed it?
Was it eighties
Girls Just Wanna Have Fun?
Was it the desolate angst of Punk?
Was it House Music?
Was it the boring dirges
of machismo Gangsta Rap?

Something got lost along the way.
SOUL? PURPOSE? ONENESS?
The changes in us were reflected
through the music we produced.

We lost the connection
between feelings, life and the music.
Our priorities changed

and were pathetically represented
in MTV presentations
of choreographed imitations
of Michael Jackson,
where lyrics were lost
in glitter and gloss,
with no substance or meaning
resulting in a reality show country
of Jerry Springer
produced and promoted
artificial anger become now real,
made for TV.
The music didn't fail us,
we failed.

Real guns aim at us again;
it ain't just four dead in Ohio.
We've become the tragic rebirth
of The Gong Show
hosted by Hannity and Limbaugh
with The Orange Man puppet
as Ringmaster!

The Who said,
"We won't get fooled again!"
but we surely were.

True Romance

(08/24/2020)

I still fantasize
running in slow motion
across the platform
at the train station in Bruges
into the arms of my lover
as she steps down
from the Paris train.
I'm still that fuckin' romantic.

Di Blasio Nightmare

(08/28/2020)

I dream I lay beside my lover
not alone for these six months.
There is intimacy
hugs are easy and warm
kisses without masks
last longer than permitted.

Stores are stocked
my fridge is overflowing
bars are filled
restaurants at capacity.
People are having fun again
and suddenly
Di Blasio's face appears
and I know
it's just a New York dream.

Moonscape

(09/06/2020)

My New York world has been dark
and devoid of moonlight
these pandemic lockdown days
but I saw the moon tonight
from the FDR.
It was illuminating!

Been missin' that craggy lunar face
with his blank stare,
but it's good to know
he's still there
that Man in the Moon,
watchin' all this crazy
goin' on down here.

I'm guessin' he's hopin'
we don't go back there
any time soon.
He surely don't need our shit.

When Did Hope Die?

(09/14/2020)

When did hope die?
Was it when he said
China was handling it?

Was it when he put in place
an ineffectual China travel ban?

Was it when he ignored the NSA report
that this was potentially
the greatest national threat?

Was it when he said
it was a Democratic hoax?

Was it when he said
it would disappear
after fifteen cases?

Was it when he said
it would just disappear
with the warm weather?

Was it when he said
we needed to reopen the country
to save the economy?

Was it when government agencies
lied to us to make him look good?
Or was it his refusal to acknowledge
190,000+ dead Americans so far
on his watch?

How many lives could have been saved
with a real leader?

Still, I Dream

(09/14/2020)

Can poetry define 2020?
We are contained.
Words are evaporated.
The muse is in absentia.
We remain lost
in a pandemic malaise
yet still I dream.

We Live

(09/15/2020)

New York City is not dead!
As long as I am alive,
the city heart beats with mine.
We are one!
Leave if you must.
You will not be missed.

Serenity

(For Andy Clausen & Pamela Twining)
(09/16/2020)

Poet friends Andy and Pamela
seem to have found serenity
at their home and garden
in Woodstock.

Here in the city,
in the noise and clamor
of daily life
serenity is more elusive
but waits silently
in unvisited churches,
synagogues, and temples,
at museums, galleries, city parks
and at fellowship meetings
where it's offered in prayer.

Six months in quarantine
has provided for me
an unexpected gift;
time alone in silence.

After a lifetime of failed
attempts at meditation
this forced alone time,
has allowed me to shed
years of useless fears, anxieties,
expectations, and beliefs.

I find in this space
my mind can be quiet, clear, calm,
and for extended periods of time,
I am at peace.

In my youth
I wanted to change the world.
At this age I now see
that the world has changed me.
Serenity.

Empty Pages
(09/22/2020)

I am now an imagined writer
a fictional creation in a real world
yet still believing myself a writer
as the muse remains muzzled
dreaming of greener pastures
where pandemics no longer exist
and life experiences happen
with stories to be told.

She waits silent and wordless
as the body count mounts
marking time for history
while I remain
lost on empty pages.

Unmasked

(09/23/2020)

Fuhgeddaboud body shaming.
Hey, I'm past that shit now.
In the East Village
it's the mask thing
that's eatin' on me.

Yeah, sure, his bod looks great,
I'm good with the Chuck Taylor's,
the Ramones T-shirt,
that all-black Punk shit,
but what's with the face?

Does he have a chin?
Is his nose too big or hooked?
Does he have zits all over his face?
Is he missin' teeth
or maybe
he's just plain butt ugly.

I can't tell anymore.
I'm gettin' confused

and I ain't willin' to take a chance
on a good-lookin' bod hunk
without a peek behind the mask first,
so no more street hookups for me here.

Goin' back to Jersey where Guidos
don't wear no masks
and I can check 'em out
before I wanna let 'em touch me
down there.

Burned Out

(09/24/2020)

I've had it with the news,
I've had it with TV,
I've had it with movies,
I've had it with social media.

The pandemic isolation
has finally eaten away
the last remaining remnants
of positivity and optimism.
I just can't take any more
freakin' bad news
watching the end of my country
as I knew it to be.

My body and mind
have reached a saturation point
with the amount
of negative information
and bad news I can absorb

from a leader who dreams
of being Mussolini
but who'll never make
the trains run on time
'cause he's too incompetent
to even do that.

When the election nightmare
finally is resolved
either by law or by violence
I will hopefully be protected
on my island of civility
in New York City.

At this point
if the country crashes and burns
we've earned it;
my dreams have died.

Responsibility
(09/27/2020)

Is it failing memory
or a willful unremembering?

I awake each day
trying to recall
the names of all friends lost
these past six months.

It's becoming more difficult;
not from the sheer numbers
but from a continuing hurt
that my heart seems
unwilling to bear the burden
of mourning every day.

Someone should be responsible
but no one is.

Distracted

(12/08/2020)

I wanted to write a poem tonight
about the ecstasy of love,
the intensity of sex with my partner,
but two thousand Americans died today
and I got distracted.

I wanted to write a poem tonight
about pulling a kite string in Central Park
on a beautiful summer Sunday
but two thousand Americans died today
and I got distracted.

I wanted to write a poem tonight
about East Village dive bar friends
the music and the good times
but two thousand Americans died today
and I got distracted.

I wanted to write a poem tonight
about looking up at the New York skyline
seeing the beauty of all I love

but two thousand Americans died today
and I got distracted.

I wanted to write a poem tonight
about the fire at Middle Collegiate Church
how sad I felt
but two thousand Americans died today
and I got distracted.

I wanted to write a poem tonight
about two thousand Americans who died today
but I can't find the words.

Brothers

(12/23/2020)

We call each other
late in the night
when we've had
too much to drink.
Talkin' shit
about what we're doin'
but really
just needin' to reconnect.

We the only ones
know that shit we did.
We the only ones
remember
the shit we did.
We were there
and did that shit
and it still burns.

That time's gone now.
For everyone else,
we were never there,

never did it.
They don't know or care
anything about it no more,
but we do.

We remember that shit.
It haunts our nights.
and we call brothers
to talk shit,
bound forever
in dark memories.

Love Walks In

(12/28/2020)

Love
walks in that night
outta' nowhere,
says, "I'm back!"

I ain't lookin'
and I ain't ready,
but here comes love
swaggerin' in
like some drunk-ass sailor
sayin', "Take it or leave it, baby!"

I'm thinkin' now
I just might be game for this one,
so on a booze-soaked bar night
I call love's bluff,
and what looks at the time,
like a sure-fire train wreck,
turns out instead to be
a five-year gold bar
for two bodies tethered now
by love, romance, and poetry.

Two broken people
healed and blessed
with redemption.

On Being Post-Beat

For Vincent

(03/05/2021)

Did we ever really exist
on those open mics
in the backrooms of dive bars
where culture hungry kids gathered
to feel or pretend to feel
what art was like?

We were there then
we were links
to those past dreamers
who said it before us
and some say,
said it better than us.

But we were there
we said our truth
tried to live it
until we couldn't anymore.

Now there are new truths

wearing masks
speaking thickly
in tongues we no longer understand.

Our time is gone.
Behold a post-pandemic world.

In Dreams I Dance

(04/22/2021)

After a year
in pandemic confinement
I stare blankly in a mirror
looking for a me that was.
The previous me now forever gone,
lost in a vortex
of unimagined death charts.

What character remains
in the morning mirror?
Fragments of a sad youth reimagined?
Remnants of lovers enjoyed and gone?
Pieces of a body broken by life choices?

NO!
Bits of a life bitten and chewed well.
Memories of booze and drugs
overdone and exploited,
joys of live music heights
never again to be
now in arthritic body agonies.

Reflections of an old writer
seeking words to define a past
that remains unexplainable
and unrecoverable
except in memories
of those still here
who mouth the words
but can no longer dance the dance
yet, in dreams I dance.

The Loss of Joy
(04/26/2021)

I think it was the middle of March 2020
when joy as we knew it died.
Yeah, I'm pretty sure
it was around that time.

After this past year of horror,
joy seems now an abstract,
something hard to grasp,
unreachable to most.

Soon we'll be mostly vaxed up
and no longer wearing masks
going about trying
to jumpstart our lives
but the horror will remain
imprinted in the brain and heart
like the memory of 9/11
but worse; a lot worse.

We can't shake
the memory of loved ones

who passed alone
without a hand held,
who laid in wait
in a freezer truck
on a city list
for a funeral time.

We won't be able to read the names
every year on March 15
of all those who died
alone and uncomforted;
their numbers are just too many.

Those strong of spirit
may overcome the loss and the hurt
and may someday again
find joy in life
but it ain't comin' easy.

Joy is gonna be hard to regain;
I mean, really hard to regain
after all we've seen this past year.

Hopefully
the return of music
poetry
art
and nature
will help.

Survivor's Guilt
(05/06/2021)

I'm all vaxed up
emerging
from a year of horrors
into a new world.

I'm here now
a better person
than I was
in that other life.

I may have taken
too much for granted,
failed to "smell the roses."
as the cliché goes.

Friends, lovers,
daily activities,
were everyday expectations
but now seem new wonders
to be cherished
held close

and appreciated.

In spite of last year's decimation,
I've emerged
with a new joy for life.

Survivor's guilt?
Perhaps,
but I'm still here
expecting deliverance
so don't break out the halo.
I ain't no saint yet.

Butterfly
(08/01/2021)

The me that was
in my past life
died
during the pandemic.

That long year of aloneness
created a new caterpillar me
now emerging
in a post-pandemic life
as a butterfly
unknown, yet hopeful
and in wonder
that I may again fly.

About the author:

Phillip Giambri

Phillip Giambri left home at eighteen and never looked back. He's seen and done what others dream of or fear. That's how he lives and that's what he writes.

His 2020 novelette *The Amorous Adventures of Blondie and Boho* is a story of love, survival, and gentrification in NYC's East Village. His 2017 chapbook *Love Borne in Retrograde* is a collection of love poems and erotica and the 2016 memoir *Confessions of a Repeat Offender* is a compilation of his performance stories and poems.

Phillip was a 2020 Acker Award recipient for Storytelling and Community Service and his work has appeared in *From Somewhere to Nowhere: The End of the American Dream* (Unbearables Anthology 2017) *Eternal Snow: A Worldwide Anthology of 100 Poets* with Yuyutsu Sharma, *Home Planet News* (Issues #2 and #5), *Sensitive Skin Magazine, Artists in the Kitchen, "Walt's Corner"* (The Long Islander), *NewYorkCityTalking.com* and the prestigious *Revista de traduceri literare (Review of Literary Translations) no. 5*

(Bucharest, Romania). He was featured in a 2016 *New York Times* story/interview, *The Villager, Chelsea News*, and in 2017 on *WBAI's "Talk Back" FM* radio with Corey Kilgannon. He was also a featured poet at the historic Club A in Bucharest, Romania.

He produced and curated a popular monthly spoken word/poetry event, *Rimes of The Ancient Mariner* for five years, is *Associate Producer* Off-Broadway production of *"Intrusion"* (Written and performed by Qurrat Ann Kadwani), as well as special collaborative events with other artist/performers; *Barflies & Broken Angels, What the Hell Is Love?, The Losers Club, Are You Dangerous?, What Were the '60s Really like,? New York Story Exchange,* and *10 Penny Comedy Show.* https://www.amazon.com/Phillip-Giambri/e/B01ACGQ7HQ?ref_=dbs_p_pbk_r00_abau_000000

Made in USA - Kendallville, IN
46992_9781513684819
07.16.2022 1346